What's Up?

written by Mary Louise Bourget • illustrated by Sheila Lucas

HARCOURT BRACE & COMPANY

Orlando   Atlanta   Austin   Boston   San Francisco   Chicago   Dallas   New York
Toronto   London

What's up?

The sky is what's up.

What's in the sky?
In the daytime, the sun and the clouds—
they stay in the sky.

Birds and kites and balloons fly by.

In the nighttime, the moon and the stars—
they stay in the sky.

Bats and bugs and airplanes fly by.

Yes, but I must know—what's up?
Nothing. What's up with you?